Flying Jewels

Katacha Díaz

Contents

What Are Hummingbirds? 2

Where Do Hummingbirds Live? 4

What Do Hummingbirds Look Like? 6

How Are Hummingbirds' Feathers Special? 10

How Do Hummingbirds Eat? 12

How Do Hummingbirds Fly? 14

Index 16

Rigby

What Are Hummingbirds?

Hummingbirds are the smallest birds.
Their wings move so fast
that you can't even see them!
Their wings make a humming sound.
That's why we call them hummingbirds!

Where Do Hummingbirds Live?

Hummingbirds have homes in many places. They live all over the Americas. Many of them live where it is hot. In South America, the people call the bird *picaflor*.

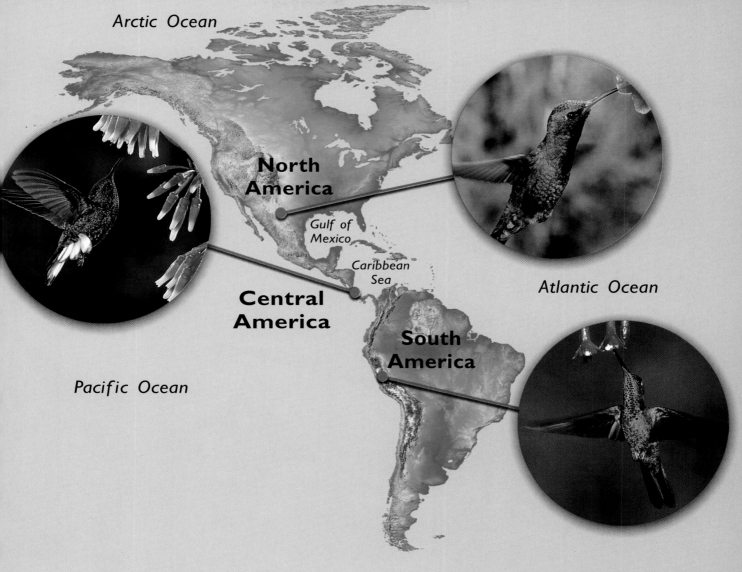

Arctic Ocean

North
America

Gulf of
Mexico

Caribbean
Sea

Central
America

South
America

Atlantic Ocean

Pacific Ocean

5

What Do Hummingbirds Look Like?

There are more than 300 kinds
of hummingbirds.
Some have special beaks and fancy tails.
Others look like they have crowns
on their heads.

The smallest hummingbird is
the Bee Hummingbird.
It is about 2 inches long.
The largest is the Giant Hummingbird.
It is about 8 inches long.

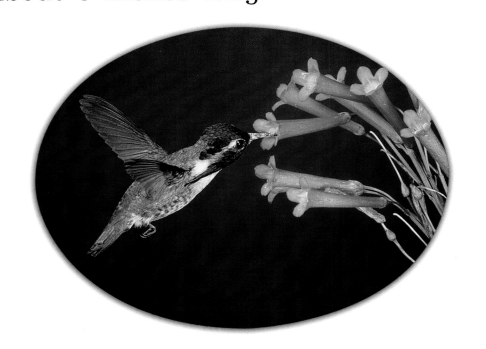

How Are Hummingbirds' Feathers Special?

Hummingbirds' feathers can be many colors. They can be green, red, purple, or orange. They can change colors!

How Do Hummingbirds Eat?

Hummingbirds' beaks are
long and thin.
They have
long tongues, too.
Hummingbirds fly
from flower to flower
to get food.

How Do Hummingbirds Fly?

Hummingbirds look funny when they fly.

Hummingbirds fly up, down, and to the side.

They also fly upside down, and they roll over!

Hummingbirds are pretty and colorful.

Some people call them flying jewels!

Index

 beaks 6–7, 12–13

 homes 4–5

 feathers 10–11

 tails 6–7

 heads 6–7

 wings 2–3